THE
MONSTER
OF LOCH NESS

JAMES CORNELL

SCHOLASTIC BOOK SERVICES

New York Toronto London Auckland Sydney Tokyo

Maps on pages 54 and 55 by Michael Jimenez

Copyright © 1977 by James C. Cornell, Jr. All rights reserved. Published by Scholastic Book Services, a division of Scholastic Magazines, Inc.

12 11 10 9 8 7 6 5 4 3 2   7 8 9/7 0 1 2/8
                Printed in the U.S.A.   06

CONTENTS

MONSTER OR MYTH?

Man-made hoax or missing link? Mysterious animal or mass hallucination? What strange wonder dwells in Loch Ness?

These questions have puzzled and intrigued scientists and public alike for more than four decades.

Loch Ness is a long, narrow lake in the Scottish Highlands (pronounced LOCK, "loch" is the Gaelic word for "lake"). Surrounded by rolling farmlands, grassy meadows, and, in many places, dark, thick woods and rough, rocky cliffs, Loch Ness has always been a scenic resort for visitors from England and abroad. In winter, however, the tourists leave the Highlands, the weather becomes cold, dark, and damp, and Loch Ness returns to its primitive, natural state, the perfect haunt for some fantastic, forgotten beast.

For the past 1,400 years, people have claimed to see such a creature in the loch. Known as "the monster," or more affectionately as "Nessie," this creature has been described variously as a giant worm, a dragon, a sea serpent, an overweight otter, an elongated eel, and, most interesting, a living fossil, a relic from the era of dinosaurs that was trapped in the lake after the last Ice Age.

Sightings have been made by scores of reliable witnesses — doctors, lawyers, clergymen, military officers. Millions of words have been written about Nessie in the world's press. Thousands of tourists have traveled to the Loch to see if they, too, could spot the beast. And several hundred amateur and professional scientists have spent innumerable hours along the lake shore hoping to capture conclusive proof of Nessie's existence on film, tape, or radar.

I went to Loch Ness in the summer of 1976, to learn about the search at first hand. I talked with the scientists working there, with the local residents, and with other experts who have been pursuing the mystery for years.

This book describes the long search for Nessie. That search still goes on, of course, and the riddle of Loch Ness could be solved any day. Perhaps, after reading this book, you will agree that Nessie could exist. Or perhaps you will develop your own theory about whether the creature is a monster — or only a myth!

J.C.
October, 1976

THE MONSTER SAGA BEGINS

The day was bright and sunny, unusual weather for the Scottish Highlands, when Mr. and Mrs. John Mackay set out by car from the little town of Drumnadrochit bound for Inverness on the new road along the north shore of Loch Ness.

Long stretches of this road had been blasted from the solid rock cliffs that dropped straight into the dark lake. The sound of dynamiting had disturbed the tranquility of this sleepy corner of Scotland for many weeks in early 1933.

Now in mid-April, the countryside was quiet again. The loch, too, seemed at rest, lying calm and smooth without even a hint of ripples.

Mrs. Mackay was surprised, therefore, to see a disturbance out on the water. "Look, John!" she cried to her husband. "What's that — out there?"

Mr. Mackay stopped the car at the side of the road overlooking the lake. He and his wife then witnessed an incredible sight.

The waters churned and boiled as if stirred up by some giant hand. As the commotion abruptly stopped, an object moved away toward the center of the lake leaving a large wave behind it.

Two large humps emerged from the water. "The rear hump appeared first," said Mrs. Mackay. "And I took it to be part of a whale because of its blue-black color. Then a second hump rose off the water and together they moved forward with a rolling motion."

According to the Mackays' account, the humps had a smooth outline with no traces of fins or other protuberances. The humps rose and fell, undulating like a garden hose being slowly jerked up and down. The humps seemed to be part of a large body about 20 feet long.

The creature — or, at least, the humps — neared the opposite shore, about one mile away from the Mackays' vantage point, and then disappeared with much splashing beneath the surface.

The Mackays sat stunned and silent. The

entire episode had taken only a few minutes, but they were certain of what they had seen: some great animal that was "no ordinary denizen of the deep."

The Mackays were owners of the Drumnadrochit Hotel; and, perhaps because they didn't want anyone to think they were seeking publicity, they made no official report of their sighting when they arrived at Inverness later that afternoon.

However, a few days later, Alex Campbell, a young, part-time correspondent for the *Inverness Courier,* tracked down the Mackays and wrote up the story, promising not to mention their name. When Campbell brought the story into the *Courier*'s offices, the editor supposedly remarked: "If this thing is as big as they say it is, we can't just call it a creature; it must be a *monster!*"

Thus, the story of the "Loch Ness Monster" appeared in the May 2, 1933, edition of the *Courier* and, within days, was reprinted in newspapers all over the globe. In a world beset by terrible economic problems (the Great Depression had crippled the United States and Europe) and the threat of war (Hitler and Mussolini were already rattling their sabres), news of something strange and mysterious in a remote Scottish lake came as refreshing relief to grim, gloomy predictions of death and destruction.

Alex Campbell's story may have focused international attention on an isolated corner of the British Isles and marked the start of the modern "monster saga." But the story was already old hat for the Highlanders. At Loch Ness, the legend of the monster called "Nessie" was already 1,400 years old.

MONSTERS OF
THE PAST

St. Columba was an Irishman who brought Christianity to Scotland some 1,400 years ago. He also met the Loch Ness Monster.

One day St. Columba was traveling along the loch on his way to visit Brude, King of the Northern Picts, at Inverness. At a ferry crossing near the modern site of Drumnadrochit (where the Mackays made their sighting), St. Columba came upon a group of Picts mourning the death of a man killed by a monster in the loch. Despite their warnings, Columba desired to cross the loch, so he ordered one of his followers to swim across the other side and bring back the boat.

According to an account of the saint's life, one of the men immediately jumped into the water. "But the monster, perceiving the surface of the water disturbed by the swimmer, suddenly came up and, moving toward the man, rushed with a great roar and an open mouth. St. Columba, observing this, raised his holy hand and invoked the name of God and formed the sign of the cross in the air and commanded the ferocious monster, saying: 'Thou shall go no further nor touch the man; go back with all speed.' At the voice of the saint, the monster was terrified and fled more quickly than if it had been pulled back with ropes."

Whether or not you believe the tales about the miracles performed by saints, it is a strange coincidence that, of all the lakes in Scotland, this meeting with a great monster 14 centuries ago occurred in Loch Ness.

Only scattered references to the monster appear over the next several centuries, perhaps because the Highlands remained an isolated corner of Britain and most stories and tales were passed by word-of-mouth rather than by written reports. But in the hills and glens around the loch the legend remained alive, and residents claimed to see it with regularity.

During the mid-17th century, when English troops occupied the Highlands to control the wild and rebellious Scottish clansmen, a gunboat regularly patrolled the loch. One of the troopers stationed there called it "the famous Loch Ness, so much discussed for its supposed floating island. . . ." Could that floating island have been some large creature basking on the surface?

In the early 1700's, the first real road was built along the north shore of Loch Ness. Construction work was under the supervision of General Wade, leader of the English troops in Scotland. (The road still bears his name today.) Several hundred soldiers worked on the project as did many English miners who blasted a way through the rocky cliffs. During this long and noisy construction project, many soldiers reported seeing strange shapes on the lake and beneath its surface. On two specific occasions they reported what appeared to be "whales" in the lake, and the men assumed that somehow these sea animals had entered the freshwater lake through subterranean passages. Were these "whales" really the mysterious Loch Ness Monster?

Around the beginning of the 19th century, a crofter (farmer) named Alexander Campbell (an ancestor of the reporter who later described the 1933 sighting), living at the village of Abriachan, saw the creature several times. Once while rescuing a lamb that had fallen over a cliff, he saw a huge creature surface in the lake and swim to within 50 yards of the shore before turning back to center lake and submerging with a great splash. Mr. Campbell saw short legs or fins on the side of the creature. He described the creature as about 20 feet long. It reminded him of a giant salamander.

In 1872, another local resident, a Mr. Mackenzie, claimed to see the creature at high noon on such a grand sunny day that "it was impossible to be mistaken. The creature looked rather like an upturned boat and went at great speed wriggling and churning up the water."

One of the more frightening tales came in 1880, from a diver working on a sunken ship near the mouth of the canal leading into the south end of Loch Ness. Soon after Duncan MacDonald was lowered into the water, he sent up a frantic signal to be pulled out. MacDonald's face was chalk white when he emerged from the water. He was trembling violently and could not find the strength to speak. Only days later could he describe his experience. He had seen some large animal lying on the shelf of rock where the wreck had gone down. "It was a very odd-looking beastie, like a huge frog." MacDonald never dove in the loch again.

Hundreds of similar tales were told by

long-time residents along Loch Ness's shores. Tales of sightings by ancestors. Tales of children warned not to play close to the shore. Tales of strange shapes, sounds, and noises seen and heard by fishermen and hunters.

Perhaps some of the stories are merely superstitions, old legends passed down from grandparents to children gathered around firesides on long winter nights. But many other stories come from reliable, sober witnesses, respected members of the community as well as outsiders with no ties to the area. Indeed, even within the past 40 years, literally thousands of people have reported seeing strange creatures in Loch Ness.

THE MONSTER
OBSERVED

"What on earth is that?" yelled Mrs. Spicer.

About 200 yards in front of the Spicers' car, a long, gray object came crashing out of the bushes and moved rapidly across the asphalt headed for the lake.

George Spicer stepped on the gas and sped toward the strange creature. But the monster — or whatever it was — disappeared into the underbrush. Spicer stopped his car and searched the bushes. The leaves and branches were broken off, and the grass was matted down as if a great cart had been pulled through the bushes. But no trace of the beast could be found. Spicer could only imagine that it had gone into the lake waters.

George Spicer, director of a large London tailoring firm, had been vacationing with his wife in the north of Scotland during the summer of 1933. They had not read any news reports about the monster supposedly seen in Loch Ness earlier that spring. On the afternoon of July 22, they were thinking of little more than the scenery as they drove along the southern shore of Loch Ness.

The sun was shining brightly, so there was no mistaking what Mr. and Mrs. Spicer saw from their car window. "It was horrible — an abomination," said Mrs. Spicer. "It didn't move like the usual reptile. Instead, its body shot across the road in jerks."

Because of a slope in the road they couldn't see the creature's lower parts. Nor did they see limbs or other means of locomotion. The body seemed to move like a roller coaster, humping up and down in a flowing motion.

"The body was about five feet high and filled the road," reported Mr. Spicer. "The length was between 25 and 30 feet. Its color could only be called a dark elephant gray. We saw no tail and I didn't notice any mouth on what appeared to be the head."

The creature was in sight for only a few seconds, but the Spicers were convinced they saw a long, thin neck that moved up

11

and down. The body was a great deal larger than the neck. The whole impression was that of "a large snail with a very long neck."

Shaken badly by their experience, the Spicers continued slowly on their way. They met a cyclist on the road and paused to tell him their story. Then they stopped in the small town of Foyers, where no one seemed much concerned by their account.

Later, George Spicer wrote to the *Inverness Courier,* claiming this was his "nearest approach to a dragon or prehistoric animal . . . Whatever it is, and it may be a land and water animal, I think it should be destroyed as I am not sure I could have tackled it."

In the summer and fall of 1933, following the original monster sighting by the Mackays, scores of other people reported seeing strange things in the lake. Obviously, some of these reports were merely panicky responses to the publicity, with observers mistaking floating logs, diving ducks, and cavorting otters for monsters.

Yet many other reports from that extraordinary year cannot be explained away so easily.

"The loch was like a mill pond and the sun [was] shining brightly," when Hugh Gray went for his usual walk along Loch Ness after church on Sunday, November

13, 1933. Gray worked at the British Aluminum Company plant in Foyers and was known to be a sober, reliable person.

"An object of considerable size rose out of the water not so very far from where I was," reported Gray. "I immediately got my camera ready and snapped the object which was two or three feet above the surface. I did not see any head, for what I took to be the front parts were under the water. But there was considerable movement from what appeared to be the tail. The object only appeared for a few minutes, then sank out of sight."

Gray couldn't estimate an exact size for the creature, but thought it was "very great." Its smooth, dark gray skin appeared to glisten in the afternoon sun.

Gray took five shots of the unknown object in the water. Then he did an odd thing. He took the camera home and locked it away in a drawer. Later, Gray would explain that he didn't think he had got anything on film because of his distance (200 yards) from the object. More important, he was afraid that he'd be laughed at by his friends at work.

Two weeks after Gray saw the creature, his brother took the film into Inverness for processing. Four of the five frames were blank, but the fifth showed a dark, eel-like shape partially obscured by clouds of spray, apparently tossed up by the movement of the creature.

The photograph appeared in the Scottish *Daily Record*, along with a description by Gray and a statement from the Eastman Kodak Company certifying that the negative had been examined by trained technicians and no evidence of retouching or tampering had been found.

Hugh Gray had made the first photograph of the Loch Ness Monster. And the reaction to its publication was instant and sensational.

The scientific community was doubtful, dubious, and downright hostile toward the photographic evidence. One researcher at the British Museum of Natural History wrote: "I am afraid the photo does not bring the mystery any nearer to a solution. It does not appear to me to be the picture of any living thing. My personal opinion is that it shows a rotting tree trunk which rose to the loch surface when gas was generated in its cells."

Another expert at Glasgow University wrote that the photo was "unconvincing as the representation of a living creature." Another said the photo could be identified as "a bottlenosed whale, one of the larger species of shark, or just mere wreckage."

If science remained unconvinced that something unusual swam beneath the dark surface of Loch Ness, the public at large certainly believed the stories. In the winter of 1933, scores of newsmen turned up at the lake seeking eyewitnesses and other possible photographic sightings of the monster. They found plenty of witnesses: Nearly 20 sightings had been made since the spring of 1933 — and more would come.

Naturally, some of these sightings were mistakes, misconceptions, and outright hoaxes. But others had the ring of truth and a reliability that could not be ignored. For example, who would have less reason to create a hoax than a respected military surgeon? And who could better know and recognize natural creatures than a veterinarian?

THE VETERINARIAN
AND THE SURGEON

Weird, shifting shadows skipped across the
deserted road. The single, jiggling headlamp of the speeding motorcycle created
strange patterns of light and darkness
ahead. Black shapes jumped off bushes and
bumps. Furry, small things scuttled
through the bouncing beam, their eyes
gleaming red and bright before disappearing into the roadside bushes.

Arthur Grant, a 21-year-old veterinary
student, was returning home after spending the evening in Inverness. It was quite
late, after midnight, for Arthur had had
mechanical troubles with his motorcycle.

As he reached a point several miles west
of Inverness on the north side of Loch Ness,

the clouds parted and the bright moon lit up the roadway. Just ahead, Arthur Grant saw a large, dark shape move out of the bushes on the right-hand side of the road.

As Grant frantically applied his brakes, the "thing" bounded across the road in two great leaps and vanished into the bushes on the other side. He jumped from his motorcycle and charged into the undergrowth after the creature. But as he reached the shore of the loch, Grant heard something go into the water with a great splash.

Grant marked the spot of his sighting and then hurried home as fast as his motorcycle could go. He immediately awakened his younger brothers and told them what he had seen. His same story later appeared in the local newspaper.

"I had a splendid view of the object. In fact, I almost struck it with my motorcycle. It had a long neck and large oval-shaped eyes on top of a small head. The tail was five to six feet long and very powerful; it did not come to a point. The total length of the animal was between 15 and 20 feet.

"Knowing something of natural history I can say that I have never seen anything in my life like the animal I saw. It seemed a cross between a giant seal and a plesiosaur."

(Grant's description of the creature as a "plesiosaur" was the first suggestion that the Loch Ness Monster might be a prehistoric relic from the age of dinosaurs. The theory is still believed, and we'll discuss it in more detail later.)

"It had a head rather like an eel or a snake, flat on top, with a longish neck and somewhat larger tail. The body was thicker toward the tail than the front portion. It was black or dark brown and had a skin rather like a whale."

Grant was less clear about the underbelly of the creature, or what its limbs had looked like, probably because his motorcycle's single, unsteady headlamp wasn't bright enough to illuminate clearly all the animal as it rushed across the road.

Grant's sighting caused a major flap in Scotland. Unfortunately, his observation came right on the heels of a silly hoax at Loch Ness, and many people thought his story was another fraud. However, Grant stuck by his account; and his sighting is still considered one of the most reliable, as well as the best proof that the creature may sometimes come ashore.

In April, 1934, Col. Robert Kenneth Wilson, a London surgeon, came to the Highlands for a hunting vacation. He brought along a camera equipped with telephoto lens so he might take photographs of wild fowl and trains, two of his special interests.

Early one morning, as he and a friend drove along the north shore of Loch Ness, they stopped on a small cliff above the lake to enjoy the view. A commotion on the lake surface about 200 yards away from the shore caught their attention. The two men watched for about a minute or so. Then, something broke the surface. "My God, it's the Monster!" shouted his friend. Col. Wilson ran back to the car and grabbed his camera from the seat. Scrambling down the steep bank, he hurriedly focused on the object in the water, and in two minutes snapped off four quick shots before the object disappeared.

Driving on to Inverness, the surgeon went straight to a drug store and left the film to be developed. He told the druggist that he thought he might have photographed the Monster. That afternoon the film was ready.

The first two exposures were blank. But on the third there was a positive image.

Although out of focus and somewhat cloudy, that image is still unmistakable: a thin, curving neck arches up and out of the water and ends in a small snakelike head. The object looks very much like a reptile with its head raised ready to strike. In fairness, it also looks like a swan or other long-necked bird floating on the water.

(Many scientists claim that, indeed, the

"creature" is *only a bird*. Or the tail of a large otter. Or merely a half-sunken log!)

The fourth exposure on the film roll showed what appears to be the tip of this neck and head at the moment the creature began to submerge. Comparison of the two exposures certainly indicates the same object is in both.

The existence of these two photos in sequence at least argues that the creature was not a bird, or it would appear to be flying away. Nor could it have been a diving otter, since there hardly would have been time for two shots.

Forty years later, the famous photograph was sent to the National Aeronautics and Space Administration for study by the same photo-enhancement techniques used to improve the clarity of pictures taken from spacecraft. The tests proved the photo had no signs of tampering or retouching. The improved images also showed clearly a pattern of ripples at the rear of the neck, indicating the presence of a larger body beneath the water. More interesting, perhaps, the NASA technicians also saw traces of "whiskers" sprouting from the creature's lower jaw.

Oddly enough, Col. Wilson, himself, never claimed to have photographed the Monster. But his picture, now known simply as the "Surgeon's Photograph," is the most famous ever taken of the elusive creature.

The appearance of the "Surgeon's Photo," plus the scores of eyewitness accounts, convinced many naturalists that some large creature of an undetermined nature could be living in Loch Ness. Beginning in 1934, a series of research expeditions would probe the lake depths in search of the mysterious "Monster." Unfortunately, few of the eager investigators realized what a difficult job they had set for themselves. Loch Ness does not give up its secrets easily.

THE STAGE
FOR A MYSTERY

Loch Ness is the perfect stage for a mystery.
When the sun shines and weather is warm,
Loch Ness can be a gentle, peaceful place.
Herds of lazy black and white dairy cows
graze quietly in rolling meadows. Green
hills cleared for farming look at a distance
like huge overstuffed pillows. Tiny pleasure boats skitter gaily across its waters.

But when the weather changes, so does
the mood of Loch Ness. The waters turn
inky black and brooding. The lake seems to
stretch as far as the eye can see, almost as if
the water was flowing into eternity. Clouds
cast strange shapes on the surface. Unexplained waves appear abruptly out of

nowhere. The lake seems cruel and frightening.

Loch Ness is an unsettling place to visit. The neat farmlands and picturesque little villages are in sharp contrast with the thick woods, steep cliffs, and deep dark glens. By turns serene and sinister, the mood of Loch Ness changes every minute without warning. The sense of peace and quiet becomes one of dread and fear. The changeable, unpredictable nature of Loch Ness is caused by its unusual physical characteristics. And the same features that create this atmosphere of calm mixed with danger also create serious problems for anyone seeking creatures living in its depths.

Some 300 to 400 million years ago, a violent shift in the giant block of land making up the continent of Europe wrenched northern Scotland apart from the rest of Britain. A huge crack in the earth created what is now known as the Great Glen of Scotland, a deep trench running from Inverness on the east coast to Loch Linnhe on the west. The sea rushed in to fill the glen with water and what is now Loch Ness became part of the North Sea.

Over and over again, for millions of years, as whole classes of animals evolved, lived, and became extinct, the polar ice caps expanded and contracted, covering and uncovering Scotland with great sheets of ice.

Some 20,000 years ago, the last of these huge glaciers pushed south from the North Pole to cover Scotland with a layer of ice and snow some 4,000 feet deep. The final Ice Age had begun.

As this glacier retreated, it gouged the Great Glen even deeper. The glacier also left behind tons of sediment, massive amounts of rocks and dirt, that cut off the Great Glen's opening to the sea. Loch Ness had been created.

Today, Loch Ness is a narrow, steep-sided lake, some 24 miles long and up to one-and-one-half miles wide. It is the largest freshwater lake in Great Britain and the third deepest in Europe. Along much of its shoreline, rocky cliffs drop straight into the waters.

Most of the loch is more than 700 feet deep, but tests in 1969 showed that some places may be as deep as 975 feet. In still other parts, the true depths have never been recorded. The bottom of the lake is apparently "as flat as a bowling green," and its underwater sides may be pocked with thousands of caves.

The waters of Loch Ness are fresh and unpolluted, but they are hardly clear. The streams and brooks emptying into the lake run through thick layers of peat moss on the hillsides. (Local residents still cut, dry, and burn this "turf" in their fireplaces.) Billions of microscopic peat particles hang suspended in the waters of the lake, staining it the color of thick, black coffee. Visibility beneath the surface is limited to only a few feet. Fifty feet below the surface all light is filtered out, and the underwater world becomes a place of constant darkness. Many divers describe their experiences in Loch Ness as eerie, unpleasant, frightening.

Loch Ness is also very cold, with the water temperature dropping rapidly just beneath the surface. At depths below 150 feet, the temperature remains at a nearly constant 42 degrees Fahrenheit, winter and summer.

The climate of the Highlands is generally cold and damp throughout much of the year. (Scotland lies at the same latitude as Labrador and Hudson Bay in Canada; thus it experiences the same long summer days and long dark winter nights.) Yet, the loch never freezes, probably because of its great depths and its large volume of water.

The major city on Loch Ness is Inverness, the self-proclaimed "capital of the Highlands," at the northeastern end of the lake. Inverness is a modest-sized city, a bustling place in the summer when thousands of tourists arrive for sightseeing, hunting, and fishing vacations. At the southwestern end of the loch is Fort Augustus, a sleepy little town dominated by an abbey and school run by Catholic monks. Many small hamlets and villages dot the shore of Loch Ness, all sporting hotels, guesthouses, and souvenir shops.

One favorite stopping place for visitors on the north shore is Drumnadrochit. Here the shoreline is indented by a small bay where two rivers empty into the loch. On the south shore of this bay is the loch's most famous landmark, Urquhart Castle, which sits ruined and menacing like some shattered sentinel scanning the lake for enemies — or strange beings!

Until about 200 years ago, the Highlands remained isolated and remote from the rest of Britain. It was a wild, rugged area where few travelers ventured unless they were heavily armed and ready to fight. The hills abounded with wildlife — hairy Highland oxen, giant red deer, golden eagles, and wildcats. The hills and glens were ruled by the Scottish clans, fierce warrior-hunters who wore colorful plaid kilts and played wailing bagpipes. They challenged all outsiders and swore undying devotion to the dream of an independent Scotland free from English rule.

When the rebellion of 1746, led by Bonnie Prince Charlie, "pretender" to the English throne, failed, his Scottish followers were massacred at Culloden on the moors east of Inverness. English troops moved into the Highlands to crush the rebellious clans forever.

Thereafter a garrison was established at Fort Augustus and troops spread out through the glens, slaughtering men, women, and children, stripping the chieftains of their power, and selling clan lands to sheep-herding Britons from the south. By act of Parliament the wearing of clan plaids was banned in Scotland.

General Wade, leader of the English garrison, supervised construction of the first road, a dirt track running along Loch Ness's south shore from Fort Augustus to Inverness. This road exists today. Although now paved and graded, it is still an exciting trip by car, skimming over high hills to give panoramic views of the lake below, dipping into wooded glens, or cutting through desolate and deserted moors. For much of its length, the road is single lane, with small pull-out spots where cars may pass each other.

The first real opening of Loch Ness to outside visitors, however, did not come until construction of the Caledonian Canal in 1822. The canal joined the three freshwater lakes of the Great Glen, Loch's Ness, Oich, and Lochy, to form a 60-mile waterway cutting across mid-Scotland and linking the North Sea with the Atlantic Ocean. The canal has been improved several times since the 1800's, and it allows fishing boats, cabin cruisers, and the small pleasure boats of vacationers to travel freely up and down Loch Ness.

In the 1930's, a new two-lane highway was built along Loch Ness's north shore, linking Fort Augustus with Inverness via Drumnadrochit and Urquhart Castle. Many experts think the extensive dynamite blasting necessary to cut this road out of the rock cliffs may have disturbed creatures living on the bottom of the loch, thus causing the sudden rise in sightings after 1933. This new road hugs the shoreline for most of its distance. By contrast, most of General Wade's road ran through woods and behind hills so that the lake remained hidden to travelers. Perhaps the new, clear view of the lake also provided opportunities for fresh sightings of the creatures in the water.

Many first-time visitors to Loch Ness are surprised by its size. For some reason, people think Loch Ness will be as small as a country pond and that the Monster should be easily spotted floating on its surface. They also wonder how, with so many tourists coming to Loch Ness each summer, the Monster could escape detection. One reason is the loch is vast and its true depths still remain unmeasured. Worse yet, the waters are dark and cold. Locating anything in the lake — even a giant monster — is extremely difficult, as most serious investigators discovered long ago.

Another question asked by visitors is: "Why does only Loch Ness have a monster?" Shouldn't other lakes have the same kind of creatures? Well, in fact, Loch Ness is not the only lake with strange animals in its waters. Lake monsters have been reported from elsewhere in Scotland — and the world — for centuries!

A MONSTER
CALLED MORAG

The fishing smack carrying Duncan
McDonnell and William Simpson home-
ward chugged slowly over the calm surface
of Loch Morar. The lingering twilight of
this summer evening in 1969 had turned
both sky and water the color of blood.

As evening light began to fade and the air
became colder, Simpson went below to fix a
pot of tea. McDonnell remained at the
helm. A strange noise in the waters behind
the boat made him turn his head just in
time to see a huge object moving toward the
boat. It struck with an impact so violent the
tea kettle fell from the stove with a crash.
McDonnell grabbed an oar to fend off

whatever was attacking the boat. The oar snapped in two.

"Quick, bring the gun!" McDonnell yelled below.

Simpson rushed on deck with a loaded rifle and fired point blank at the shape in the water. The creature — thing? — immediately sank beneath the surface and disappeared. Shaking and frightened, the two men made for the shore as fast as their old boat would allow.

Back on land, the two men reflected on what they had seen. "It was 20 to 30 feet long," McDonnell told reporters. "The skin was rough and hard and a dirty brown color." No tail was seen, but McDonnell swore the animal had a snakelike head, about a foot wide, that rose some 18 inches out of the water on a thin neck.

Loch Morar is located about 70 miles southwest of Loch Ness in one of the most rugged and remote parts of the Highlands. It is the deepest lake in the British Isles, 300 or more feet deeper than Loch Ness, and its extreme depths have never been explored.

Also, unlike Loch Ness, the shores of Morar are generally unpopulated. A very rough, one-lane track runs only a few miles along its north side connecting the tiny settlement of Bracora with the town of Morar on the main highway. The rest of the loch is surrounded by woods and barren hills.

This remote and forbidding area is the traditional home of the McDonnell Clan; and, according to legend, whenever a member of this clan is about to die, the monster will appear in the loch. That monster is named Morag.

Sightings of Morag have been reported for centuries. In fact, one ancient Scottish song goes:

> Morag, Harbinger of Death
> Giant swimmer in deep-green
>   Morar
> The loch that has no bottom
> There it is that Morag the
>   monster lives.

In the summer of 1946, children from a summer camp were on a boat excursion across Loch Morar. Suddenly, one of the children cried out, "Oh, look! What is that big thing on the bank over there." The boat owner, Alexander McDonnell, reported seeing an animal about the size of an elephant plunge off the rocks into the water with a tremendous splash.

Two years later, a boat full of tourists on a day trip around the loch saw something following in the wake of the boat. The captain later described it as a creature "about 30 feet long, with four humps sticking two feet above the surface." He could see no head or tail, since the creature was more than a half-mile away and disappeared from view in less than a minute. But there was no mistake: "It was Morag."

In September, 1948, an English scientist named Cecil Cooper and his family camped out on the shores of Morar. One afternoon, Dr. Cooper sat painting a watercolor view of the loch's western end when he spotted what seemed to be a large log drifting on the otherwise calm waters. Unlike a log, however, this object seemed to move up and down. Cooper executed a quick watercolor sketch — the only known portrait of the Morag.

In July, 1969, Bob Duff, a regular summer visitor to Loch Morar, was out in his small boat, trolling for fish in Meoble Bay. Here the water was no more than 16 feet deep and extremely clear. Even dead leaves could be seen lying on the white sand below.

Imagine Duff's surprise, then, when he looked over the side of the boat and saw a "monster lizard lying on the bottom." The 20-foot-long creature lay motionless on the sand staring straight up at him.

Duff turned on the throttle full blast and sped away from the bay. But he remembers well seeing a snakelike head with a wide mouth and slitlike eyes. The creature seemed to be four-legged, with three large toes on each foot. The grayish brown body had a rough skin with a texture Duff described as like "burnt coke."

Obviously, some kind of creature lives in Loch Morar. What it is, no one knows. An intensive investigation has been conducted there for the past several years in an attempt to photograph the mysterious Morag.

I visited Loch Morar in the summer of 1976. Driving down the narrow one-lane road along the shore from the village, I felt as if I had entered another world. Heavy clouds clung to the hilltops on either side of the lake, turning the waters a steely gray. A light mist had been falling all day and even the hundreds of white sheep grazing on the hills seemed to glisten with tiny drops of moisture. The green pastures beside the road had become soggy bogs where a car would sink up to its axles.

The road ended in a farmyard. I got out, scattering chickens and sheep before me, and continued on foot over a rocky path through a sparse forest to a large, open, flat field bordering the lake. A few rubber boats were drawn up on the shore and, in the shelter of some trees beneath one of the surrounding hills, a few tents had been pitched.

A tall, bearded man wearing a sailor's cap came across the field to meet me. Although it was late July, he was bundled against the wet chill in a heavy, blue navy jacket.

"Hello, I'm Adrian Shine," he said, extending his hand, "Welcome to the Loch Morar Expedition."

Shine introduced me to members of his crew, who were gathered around a rough-hewn table taking their lunch, and to Nick Witchell, an authority on the search for lake creatures and the author of the excellent history, "The Loch Ness Story." Witchell was spending the summer of 1976 shuttling back and forth between the investigations at Loch Ness and Loch Morar.

While international attention focused on Loch Ness, Shine's team had been carrying out extensive investigations at Morar with little publicity and little support. His crew was all volunteer, primarily college students from Great Britain who could spend a week or two in the Highlands searching for Morag. Some 100 students were involved during the summer of 1976. They usually came in groups of ten to a dozen and worked for two- or three-week periods before being replaced by another group willing to camp out under the usually cold and rainy skies of northern Scotland.

Shine felt that his team's isolation and lack of attention was an advantage. At Morar, they were free from the troublesome bother of tourists and newsmen, and had few incidents of hoaxes or embarrassing misinterpretations of natural phenomena.

Loch Morar has another big advantage over Loch Ness. The waters of Morar are exceptionally clear, without the blurring, obscuring peat stains found in Ness.

"Our expedition uses techniques that exploit this water clarity," Shine said. "We are attempting direct underwater observation of the creature. Beneath the surface, it should be possible to see and photograph the animal's *entire profile*, not just a series of humps poking through the waves."

Between 1972 and 1975, the Morar expedition positioned small diving bells fitted with cameras at strategic points around the lake, primarily in the shallow bays where streams flowed into the lake and where the fish life was most abundant. The researchers felt any large fish-eating creature would most likely be found in these areas. The team also used a glass-bottomed boat, the *Pequod*, to search the lake bottom for bones or any other remains of the creature. When I visited them, they had added a new tool: two highly sensitive television cameras mounted in 80 to 100 feet of water and pointing straight up. Team members back on dry land constantly monitored the television screens in hopes of catching an image of a large creature swimming above the sunken cameras. By the end of the summer of 1976, the elaborate system had still not photographed Morag. But Shine was not discouraged.

"We think we are hunting the same kind of animal seen at Loch Ness," says Shine. "And often several years pass without any sighting of Nessie. The same thing may happen at Morar, because the same conditions exist here. If a creature exists in Loch Ness, then one could — in fact, should! — exist in other similar lakes as well."

Indeed, several other lakes in the Highlands do have a tradition of lake monsters. Several miles south of Morar, at Loch Shiel, other Highlanders have reported seeing a monster for many years. The creature's name is Seileag.

Loch Shiel is a long thin lake stretching southwest from the village of Glenfinnan toward the Atlantic Ocean. Glenfinnan, itself, is so isolated that it remains the only community in the British Isles without television reception.

Tales of Seileag have been told in this remote and thinly settled glen for years. For example, there is an old gameskeeper who watched the creature through a telescope. He described it as larger than a three-man boat, with a long neck, a broad wide-mouthed head, and seven "sails," or humps, along its rough-skinned back.

Equally fascinating are the reports from

Loch Oich, a small lake between Loch Lochy and Loch Ness in the Great Glen that is linked to both by rivers and canals.

According to legend, many years ago, some children playing beside a deep pool on the river emptying into Oich saw a "huge beastie in the shape of a deformed pony appear in the waters."

Curious about this strange creature, the children went closer to see if it really was a horse coming from the water. Supposedly, one of the children climbed on the creature's back and clung to the manelike growth on its neck. Suddenly, the "beastie" dived into the water taking the unfortunate child with it. No trace of animal — or child — was ever found.

Fact? Folklore? Or is this merely a scary story told by parents to keep their children away from the water's edge?

The incredible story might be dismissed, except that other, more believable sightings of a strange creature in Loch Oich also have been reported. One day in 1933, for example, the lockkeeper for the canal leading to Loch Ness was called outdoors by his daughter's shouts. Together, they witnessed an animal, about six feet long, swimming in a small cove near the house. The lockkeeper sent his daughter for the rifle, but before she could run to the house and return, the creature had disappeared.

The lockkeeper claimed it looked something like an otter — only much, much larger.

In the summer of 1936, A. J. Robertson was lazily paddling along in the calm waters near the southwestern end of the lake. The waters around his boat suddenly began to churn and boil. A huge, black, snakelike body with humps rose to the surface. The creature had a long, graceful neck and a huge, ugly head, that looked vaguely like a large dog. The creature, whatever it was, disappeared as suddenly as it had appeared.

The close connection between Loch Oich and Loch Ness certainly suggests that the same creature — or creatures — could be found in both lakes. The same holds true for the other lochs of Scotland, since all these hundreds of lakes were formed at the end of the same glacial period. The same species of prehistoric sea creatures — if that is what they are — could have become landlocked prisoners in several lakes at that same time.

Perhaps it is not so strange, then, that lake creatures have been seen in many other parts of the world where deep lakes were formed by the last Ice Age.

IRISH LAKE MONSTERS

The three priests had come down from Dublin for a short fishing vacation at Lough Ree on the River Shannon in Ireland's midlands. It was a fine, windless May evening in 1960. The long twilight of Irish spring provided plenty of light.

The three men scanned the lake surface for signs of trout rising. Suddenly one of the party exclaimed: "Look quick! Do you see what I see?"

Less than 100 yards away from their boat, a large animal swam across the water.

"It was moving up and down under the water in the form of a loop," one of the priests later reported. "The length from the end of this coil to the head was some six feet.

About 18 inches of head and neck stretched over the water. The head was flat like a python's and the neck seemed about the thickness of good-sized salmon."

Later, the priests prepared a more detailed report for Irish officials. They described seeing two sections of the creature above water; the first, or head part, stuck straight out of the water at an angle to the surface. The second part seemed to be "a tight, roughly semi-circular loop, like a hump or large knob on the back of a large body."

The creature's movement was steady and there was no disturbance on the surface, so the priests assumed it was propelled from below. Cruising at a leisurely pace, with apparently little concern for the boatload of priests, the creature swam toward the shore, submerged gradually without diving, and then reappeared briefly before sinking from view completely.

When Alphonus Mullaney, a teacher in the small Galway town of Glinsk, and his young son headed down to Lough Dubh on a late March afternoon in 1962, they planned only a little fishing expedition for perch or pike. What they caught was a monster!

"I let the boy fish with the long rod and I used a shorter rod with worm bait," Mullaney later told a newspaper reporter for the *Sunday Review*. "After a few minutes I decided the fish were not there that evening, but I took the long rod and walked up and down the bank anyhow.

"Suddenly, there was a tugging on the line. I thought it had caught on a root, so I took it gently. It didn't give. I hauled it slowly ashore and the line snapped. I was examining the line when the lad screamed.

"Then I saw the animal. It was not a seal or anything I had ever seen before. It had thick, short legs and a hippo face. It was as big as a cow and square-faced with small ears and a white pointed horn on its snout. It was dark gray and covered with bristles or short hair like a pig."

Mr. Mullaney thought the animal, or whatever it was, may have been hooked by the line and, in its pain, had tried to climb the bank and attack them. Mullaney and his son ran to the town and returned with other men armed with guns. But the creature had gone.

Tales of lake monsters abound in Irish history and legend. And perhaps it is not surprising when you look at the landscape of that little island. Along the western coast, in the Connemara, Mayo, and Kerry peninsulas, the barren land is laced with lakes of all sizes.

These lakes have shaped the lives of the Irish: forming natural boundaries, defining pastures, and providing bog lands that are sources of fuel for homes and fodder for livestock. However, in this lonely and deserted area, these same bogs and lakes can be dangerous and deadly traps into which a solitary traveler, isolated shepherd, or late-working farmer may fall and drown, his body never to be found by family or friends.

Not surprising, then, that myths and legends have grown up around these lakes — and the strange creatures that may lurk there. Some of the animals are said to be harmless: great hairy dogs that emerge from the waters to be tamed and trained, strapping water horses put to the plow, and gentle water cows that could be milked to feed poor families. But not all the legendary lake animals are so kind.

Although St. Patrick supposedly drove all the snakes from Ireland, he also was said to have chained the most terrible serpents to the lake bottoms. Every seven years, according to legend, these animals emerge to do great destruction and harm to the countryside.

But are these stories only legends? Many reliable, sober, and respectable people, such as the three priests and the schoolteacher Alphonus Mullaney, have claimed to have seen *real* creatures, not just fanciful creations of the imagination.

43

Physically, Ireland, and particularly its western coast, looks much like the Scottish Highlands. Indeed, the island was created by the same geological and weather conditions that shaped Scotland. Violent earthquakes millions of years ago stretched and broke the western coastline into a series of narrow peninsulas and deep valleys. The glaciers of the Ice Ages gouged out hundreds of deep, narrow lakes, or loughs (also pronounced "lock"), perfect homes for strange animals.

But Ireland and Scotland are not the only countries where lake monsters have been seen. Around the globe, in many other countries at the same latitude as Ireland and Scotland, that is, at approximately the same distance from the polar regions, creatures have long been reported as existing in deep lakes. Is this merely a coincidence? Or, did the Ice Age cut off certain animals from the sea, thus creating a new species of giant lake creatures?

SOE-ORM, SKRIMSL, OGOPOGO, AND SLIMEY SLIM

When Martin Olsson retired from his job in the Ostersund sawmill, he took up residence on the shore of Sweden's Lake Storsjo so he could spend most of his time fishing.

One summer day in 1874, while alone in his boat near Forso Island, he had the eerie feeling that someone — or something — was watching him. "I looked around and there was the lake creature no more than 40 yards behind me," he said.

So surprised he dropped his pole and line into the water, Olsson stared in wonder at a grayish brown creature with a long neck almost as thick as a man's body. A hairy fringe hung down its back and two large dark humps were visible. The creature's red eyes stared back directly at him.

"I didn't want to alarm the beast," he explained. "But I did want to get away as quickly as possible." Olsson began pulling slowly on his oars, edging cautiously toward the shore. The creature followed him. Olsson was filled with fear. Obviously, this creature could easily overturn his boat. But then, as suddenly as it appeared, the creature disappeared beneath the water, leaving Olsson alone and shaken.

Martin Olsson's visit from the creature in Lake Storsjo — he called it a "sea serpent" — is only one of dozens of reports of strange reptilelike creatures seen in Scandinavia. The folklore and legends of the Scandinavian people are filled with tales of great Soe-orms, or sea snakes, seen in the lakes and along the coasts of Sweden, Norway, and Iceland. In fact, the Viking ships usually had their bowsprits carved in the shape of fierce dragons and serpents.

But Martin Olsson's sighting, as well as the score of other eyewitness reports at Lake Storsjo, suggests the creature there might be more than just a legend.

In 1898, Dr. Peter Olsson, a zoologist who taught science at the Ostersund State High School (and no relation to Martin), set about collecting and investigating the many reports about Storsjo's mysterious monster.

Based on an analysis of these reports, Dr. Olsson developed a possible description. The creature, or creatures, was 15 to 40 feet long, with a grayish black, humped upper body and a lighter underbelly. It had a round, doglike head with large oval eyes, a wide mouth, and a mane or fringe of hair behind the ears. Propelled by either fins or short, powerful legs, the creature sometimes swam at speeds up to 45 miles per hour. The creature appeared most often during calm, pleasant weather. (Of course, observers are also most likely to be on the lake when the weather is good.) Although the beast had never been seen eating, it probably fed upon the fish in the lake.

Most observers felt the animal was merely curious, not dangerous or hostile, raising its head from water when some noise or commotion on the surface attracted its attention. No one ever reported any attacks by the creature, although it once gave out a terrible roar when some young girls threw stones at it.

Olsson suggested the creatures might have been some species of giant, long-necked seal. However, no such animal has ever been found in the lake. The creature has been seen many times since Olsson's research three-quarters of a century ago, most recently in 1965, but no further investigation has been conducted.

This is a shame, because in many ways the description of the Soe-orm of Lake Storsjo sounds very similar to the monster of Loch Ness. And it is also similar in description to a creature called "Skrimsl" reported living in the lakes of Iceland.

The Lagarflot is a long, narrow freshwater lake set among the geysers, volcanoes, and glaciers of eastern Iceland. Almost from the beginning of recorded history, large creatures have been seen in this lake. One chronicle from 1345 speaks of "the wonderful thing in Lagarflot which is believed to be a living animal. At times it appears as a great island and at others there appear three humps with water between them. . . ."

In the 19th century, two European travelers to this desolate area wrote to friends that they had seen the Skrimsl and that it measured "46 feet long, including a head and neck some six feet in length." Sketches of Skrimsl made by local residents show a creature with a long, humped body, a thin tail, and, most remarkable, a bewhiskered head much like a seal's.

Thousands of miles across the Atlantic, in the wilds of Canada and the northern United States, lake creatures have been seen and feared from the time of the Indians until today. Not suprisingly, the lakes of this region were also created by the last Ice Age.

Lake Okanagan is located on the Pacific side of the Rocky Mountains in the Canadian Province of British Columbia. The lake is long and narrow, stretching some 69 miles, but measuring only three-quarters of a mile to two miles wide.

When the first white settlers came to this area they found that the local Indians revered — and feared — a monster spirit of the lake known as "Naitaka." Whenever the braves ventured out on the lake, they carried with them a chicken or a small dog to be tossed into the water as an offering for the monster.

Although most pioneers thought little of this Indian legend, some settlers continued the tradition of making small offerings to the lake spirit — especially after some strange doings occurred in the lake. Several residents described seeing a large, black, humped-back shape floating on the waters. Others saw a gruesome, goatlike head poke from the water. One farmer claimed two horses were mysteriously snatched from a tow line behind his boat. The settlers called this monster "Ogopogo."

One of the best descriptions of Ogopogo comes from a local newspaperman in Vernon, British Columbia, who spotted the creature while boating on the lake with his family in July, 1959. "Returning from a cruise and traveling about ten miles per hour, I noticed in our wake what appeared to be the serpent," says R. H. Millar.

Picking up field glasses, Millar spotted a large, dark green creature with five humps on its broad back swimming along somewhat faster than his boat. "The head was about nine inches above the water and snakelike with a blunt nose." As the boat turned and approached the creature, which Millar called "Ogie," for short, it lowered its head and body into the lake and disappeared.

While Lake Okanagan and Ogopogo have received the most publicity, similar stories are told throughout the north country. At Lake Sushwap, also in British Columbia, the Indians talk of the sea serpent known as "Ta-Zam-A." At nearby Lake Cowichan, there is still another creature called "Tsinquaw."

Eskimo legends tell of other creatures beneath the ice of Alaskan lakes. The Cree Indians believe a serpent lives in Ontario's Lake Meminisha. At Mocking Lake in Quebec, the French-Canadian farmers and woodsmen tell of a dark brown or black animal, 12 to 18 feet long, with a round back and a large, jagged fin, that appears regularly in the waters.

Lake monsters have been reported from the American side of the border as well. Lake Champlain in upstate New York is said to be the home of a great serpent, although it has not been seen in recent years.

Wisconsin, that land of lakes, might also be called the land of lake monsters, for its history is full of tales of creatures seen in the hundreds of lakes across the state.

The monster of Bear Lake, Utah, is one of the most famous lake creatures in the United States. According to the Shoshone Indians, the creature was a serpent that often left the waters on short, stubby legs to hunt for food on the shores. The Indians also believed the creature had disappeared around 1830, shortly after the buffalo disappeared from the west. But, several white settlers reported seeing something in Bear Lake for many years after that date.

In 1860, S. M. Johnson was driving his horse and carriage along the shore of Bear Lake when he saw something he "thought to be a drowned person." Stopping and walking down to the shore, he waited for the "body" to drift in on the waves. Instead, he saw a strange animal rise out of the water. Although he could not see the creature's body, Johnson noted that its head had ears, or bunches, the size of teacups.

Several days later, three other travelers spotted some motion on the otherwise smooth lake. The strange waves turned out to be a very large animal, perhaps 90 feet long. Suddenly, the brownish animal sped across the water "faster than a steam locomotive." More amazing, right behind this huge animal came other slightly smaller creatures. In all, the witnesses saw six creatures swimming as if in formation, like a school of fish. (Oddly enough, several observers at Loch Ness have also reported seeing more than one monster at a time.)

Perhaps the most appealing American monster is "Slimey Slim," if only for its delightful name.

In the summer of 1941, more than 30 boaters and swimmers on Idaho's Lake Payette spotted what they called a "sea serpent." One person described the creature as "about 35 feet long, with a head resembling a snub-nosed crocodile." The creature moved about five miles an hour, swimming gracefully with an undulating motion like a coil whipping slowly above and below the water.

When the news of the sighting reached the press, hundreds of photographers and reporters, plus other assorted gawkers, lined the shores of Lake Payette to catch a glimpse of the hump-back monster. The local newspaper dubbed the creature "Slimey Slim" and dismissed the entire affair as a hoax. Unfortunately, Slimey Slim disappeared forever after that long, hot summer and probably was nothing but a hoax.

This one known case of a hoax can't explain the many other similar sightings from North America, Europe, Australia, even South America. At Loch Ness alone, there have been an estimated 10,000 sightings of strange animals. Surely they all can't be hoaxes or cases of mistaken identity. More likely something unexplained lives beneath the waters of Loch Ness and lakes elsewhere. Perhaps some special species of large aquatic animal has evolved in these lakes? Or perhaps prehistoric creatures have somehow survived from the age of dinosaurs.

If that last idea sounds too incredible to believe, then you haven't heard about the *coelacanth*.

Map of Scotland.

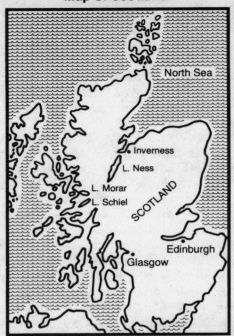

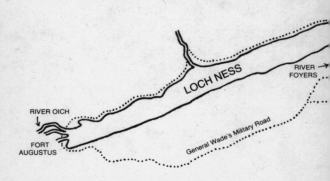

Map of Loch Ness area.

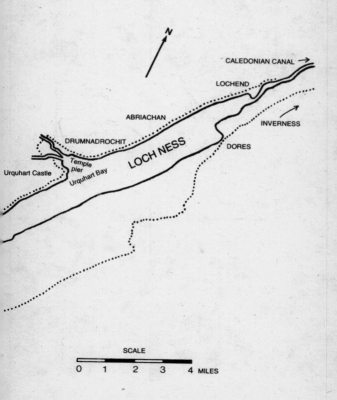

Ruins of Urquhart Castle looking northeast over Loch Ness. Photo by James Cornell.

Same ruins, looking southwest. Photo by James Cornell.

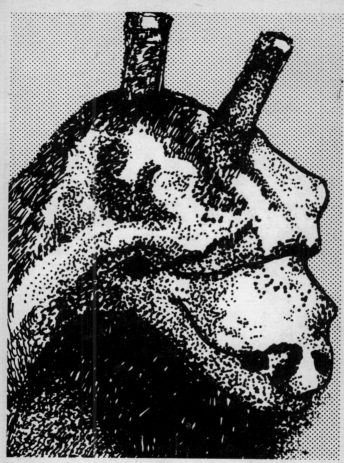

Artist's drawing based on photo made by underwater camera in Loch Ness, June 29, 1975. Copyright, Academy of Applied Science, Boston, Mass. Photo Trends

Type of creature suggested by Academy of Applied Science's photos taken at Loch Ness in 1975. Drawing by James Cornell.

Photograph of the monster taken in the mid-1930's. Wide World.

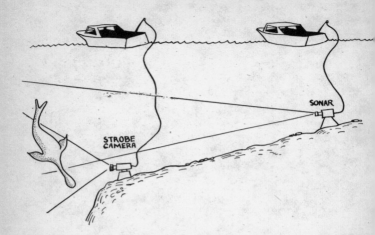

Simplified diagram of camera and sonar system used in 1970's at Loch Ness. Drawing by James Cornell.

Photograph of monster taken by strobe flash at depth of 35 feet in 80 feet or more of water in Loch Ness. Copyright, Academy of Applied Science. Photo Trends.

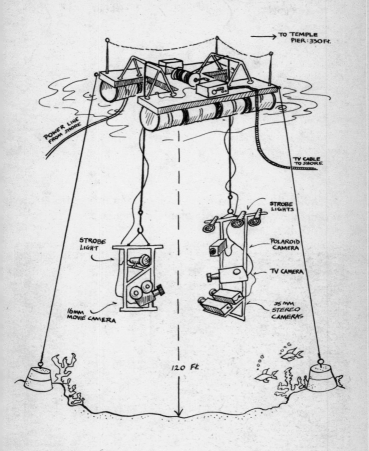

Underwater photography system used by Academy of Applied Science at Loch Ness in 1976. Drawing by James Cornell.

A claimed sighting: hump and neck appear on surface of Loch Ness in 1974. Photo Trends.

One of the many Loch Ness hoaxes: one pound of green plasticine and wire coathanger photographed in a bathtub lined with black paper and filled with water. Photo Trends.

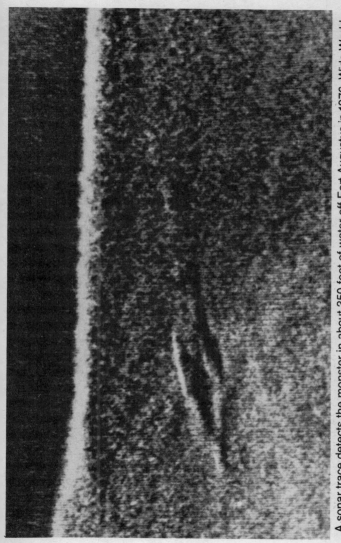

A sonar trace detects the monster in about 350 feet of water off Fort Augustus in 1976. Wide World.

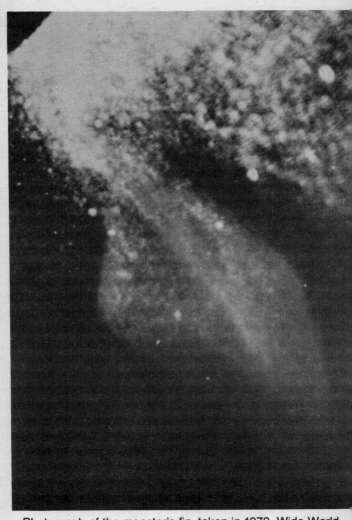

Photograph of the monster's fin, taken in 1972. Wide World.

Side-scan sonar system used at Loch Ness in 1976 to search for "monster" bones on the lake bottom. Drawing by James Cornell.

A monster from another part of the world. Believed extinct for 60,000,000 years, this Latimeria chalumnae was caught off southeast coast of Africa in 1969. It measures 4 feet in length, and weighs 92 pounds. UPI.

Artist's conception of the plesiosaur, a prehistoric marine dinosaur, often suggested as the prime candidate for a Loch Ness "Monster." Drawing by James Cornell.

Artist's conception of giant amphibian suggested by Professor Roy Mackal as possible candidate for Loch Ness "Monster." Drawing by James Cornell.

RELICS OF THE
PAST AND OTHER
POSSIBILITIES

The turbanned fishermen stared in horror at the grotesque object tangled in their net. Although battered and badly decomposed, the steely blue fish was unlike anything they had ever seen before. Some unknown monster had been dredged up from the deep ocean bottom off the coast of Madagascar.

The five-foot-long carcass was wrapped in burlap and sent to a zoologist at South Africa's Rhodes University. The astonished scientist tentatively identified the creature as a coelacanth (SEAL-uh-kanth) — a fish thought to have been extinct for 70 million years!

The world's scientific community was highly skeptical when an announcement of this discovery was made in 1938, because no one believed that a relic from the age of the dinosaurs could have survived until modern times. This fish simply cannot exist, they declared. But 14 years later, in the Indian Ocean off East Africa, a fisherman on one of the Comoro Islands pulled in another coelacanth on his hook and line. The doubting scientists had been dead wrong.

Why was this discovery so important? First, the existence of the coelacanth, a supposedly extinct species, reminded scientists that they could not afford to be so positive about any so-called "impossible phenomena." Second, if the coelacanth existed, then other prehistoric creatures might also exist at great depths in the oceans or freshwater lakes where no diver, submarine, or fishing nets had yet reached.

Most interesting for the riddle of Loch Ness, the discovery gave new support to the popular theory that Nessie could be a *plesiosaur*, a giant, fish-eating reptile that roamed the waters around Great Britain some 100 million years ago.

Certainly, the skeletal remains of the elasmosaurus, one member of the plesiosaur family, look remarkably similar to modern-day descriptions of the strange animals seen in Loch Ness and elsewhere. The elasmosaurus had a long, thin neck, a smallish, snakelike head, a long tapering tail, and four thick-limbed flippers. The plesiosaurs were about 20 feet long, swam rapidly, and gave birth to live offspring in the water.

Before settling on the plesiosaur as the best candidate for the mysterious lake monsters, however, consider some of the problems with this theory. First, all evidence indicates the plesiosaur became extinct in ocean waters some 65 million years ago. But, Loch Ness and the other inland lakes became cut off from the sea only 10,000 years ago, after the last Ice Age.

This means the plesiosaurs must have somehow survived somewhere for millions of years between the time the rest of their dinosaur cousins disappeared and the time the glaciers left Scotland. Although this sounds very difficult, the discovery of coelacanths still living on the bottom of the sea at least suggests it could have happened.

But on the other hand, if the plesiosaur somehow managed to survive in Loch Ness, would it still look the same today as it did millions of years ago? First, these saltwater creatures would have had to adapt to the freshwater environment of the lake. Second, evolutionary processes over millions of years may have given the creature a completely different physical appearance.

Thus, any similarity between the modern monsters and the fossil remains of ancient dinosaurs may be just a coincidence. Still, the survival of the plesiosaur — and its physical characteristics — could be possible, even if unlikely.

If Nessie and her cousins are not giant, prehistoric reptiles somehow related to plesiosaurs, what else could they be? Actually, as biologist Roy Mackal has pointed out in his book *The Monsters of Loch Ness*, there are several good candidates.

For example, some scientists have suggested the lake creature really might be a giant aquatic mammal, such as an otter or seal, a whale or dolphin, or even a manatee or sea cow. Large otters, or a family of otters, have often been suggested as explanations for the creatures seen at Loch Ness. However, no otter is known to dive to depths of 700 feet as reported for Nessie. Moreover, the rare surface sightings of Nessie indicate it doesn't need to breathe regularly above water. This, of course, is not true of otters.

Seals and walruses are perhaps better candidates, for they dive deeply and rapidly. However, these mammals also must surface regularly to breathe. More important, they usually give birth to their young on ice floes, which are never found in Loch Ness.

Whales and dolphins, although having the same general color and size as reported for the lake creatures, have few other characteristics in common. Obviously, they don't have long necks, humped backs, or snakelike heads.

Mackal thinks the most likely candidate among the mammals could be Steller's sea cow. This huge animal, related to the manatee (a creature itself mistaken for mermaids by ancient sailors), was once found in and around the northern seas. It had a large, elephantlike body, with a lumpy, humped back and rough skin, and a doglike face at the end of a long, thick neck. Although the sea cow spent most of its life in the water, it occasionally came ashore, much like Nessie supposedly does. The last confirmed sighting of this creature was in 1741.

The Loch Ness animals might also be some unknown species of amphibian, a classification that includes toads, frogs, newts, and salamanders. Although most amphibians known today are too small to qualify as "monsters," fossils from the Carboniferous Period, some 270 million years ago, show that huge eel-like creatures, half-fish and half-lizard, once existed. Some of these creatures are known to have survived at least until 150 million years ago. Perhaps some others have managed, like the coelacanth, to survive undetected until the present day.

Some critics of the Loch Ness theory claim the so-called monsters are really only very large fish. In fact, even many residents of the Loch Ness area think that Nessie may be a large-bodied eel. The common European eel grows as long as five or six feet, with a circumference of two feet. Conger eels and moray eels, more often found in tropical waters, grow as long as nine or ten feet.

Fishermen at Loch Ness also refer to a variety of eel known as the "hair eel" or "horse eel," a fish with a thin, filmy fin that looks like a horse's mane growing down on its back. When swimming close to the surface, this eel might even appear to have humps.

Other fish seem unlikely candidates as monsters, primarily because most large fish are saltwater denizens. More important, few species are ever on the surface long enough to produce the type of sightings reported at Loch Ness and elsewhere.

Several writers have proposed that the Loch Ness Monster might be a giant invertebrate, that is, an animal without a backbone. This classification includes squids, worms, snails, and sea slugs. For example, the American naturalist William Beebee once speculated that the monster could be a giant squid, with its tentacles accounting for both the humps and the long, thin, snakelike appearance often noted.

F. W. Holiday, a British writer, has suggested the monster could be a giant form of the *Tullimonstrum gregarium*, a prehistoric, water-going worm that has only been found as a fossil. This creature had a long, thin upper body ending in a round, bulblike head, with two flabby, leg-like appendages in its midsection, and a finned tail.

Professor Mackal believes firmly that a "population of fish-eating, aquatic animals is inhabiting Loch Ness. These animals are moderate in size relative to animal life in general, but large when compared to the known freshwater fauna." His favorite candidates for the monsters are either a huge eel or, more likely, a giant amphibian, perhaps some relative of that prehistoric lizard-fish thought extinct for the past 270 million years.

Although many biologists share Professor Mackal's view that large creatures inhabit Loch Ness, not all agree. In fact, a considerable number of people think the monster is nothing more than a mirage!

WAVES, HOAXES, AND OPTICAL ILLUSIONS

"Look quick!" Charlie Wyckoff yelled. "There's the monster!"

Sure enough, as I turned in the direction he pointed and looked along the shore of Loch Ness, a series of black humps moved rapidly across the water, rolling up and down as if a coiled beast were diving through the gentle surf. Then the black humps disappeared.

I was standing in the Academy of Applied Science's small research trailer at Temple Pier on Loch Ness in July, 1976, when photographic expert Charles Wyckoff called my attention to the monster. Only it wasn't a monster, it was an unusual wave pattern peculiar to Loch Ness.

As Wyckoff explained, the steep sides of the loch help produce a peculiar pattern of water flow known as the "standing wave." When a boat passes through the loch, it creates the normal V-shaped wave. These waves, sometimes no more than a gentle ripple, travel to the shore. But, like water sloshing in a bathtub, they bounce back toward the center of the narrow lake where they may reappear, sometimes many minutes later, as a line of turbulent water moving in almost the same direction as the passing boat. Of course, by this time, the boat has moved many yards, or even miles, away. The "standing wave" thus appears as if some object under the water is chasing the boat.

Similarly deceptive wave patterns are seen nearer the shore. The water wave flowing back toward the center may meet other incoming waves and produce a high rippling effect that looks for all the world like a series of two, three, or more moving "humps" poking around the surface. Because the lake waters are peat-stained and naturally dark, it is easy to imagine you are watching some big, black creature swimming just beneath the surface. This is what I had seen.

How many other people have been fooled by this optical illusion into thinking they have seen the monster? It is impossible to estimate.

The professional monster hunters, such as Wyckoff, Mackal, and the members of the Loch Ness Investigation Bureau (more about their activities in the next chapter), keep accurate records of boats and other unnatural activity on the lake so they won't be confused by these waves. However, the first-time visitor — and even some long-time residents — can be easily fooled. In fact, even while I visited with Wyckoff, a tourist couple brought in some pictures taken a few days earlier that they were sure showed the monster clearly. Unfortunately, they had only snapped the "standing wave" effect.

Some skeptics claimed *all* the sightings at Loch Ness were either similar cases of mistaken identity — or outright hoaxes. One popular theory, offered by scientists immediately following the first sighting more than 40 years ago, suggested the monster was really a "large lump of water-logged peat floating around Loch Ness at the mercy of wind and currents."

Other naturalists say the sudden appearance and disappearance of the "monster" may be caused by the rise and fall of decaying logs. Water-soaked and rotten, the tree trunks might lie undetected on the lake bottom for years. As the wood decays, however, trapped gas could cause the log to rise to the surface. Once on top of the lake, the gases escape and the heavy log sinks again.

A variety of biologists have suggested that many sightings can be explained as large otters playing the water, or as flocks of water birds, or even as stags swimming across the loch. (The giant red deer, extinct throughout most of England, can still be found in the Highlands.)

Naturally, many other people claim that the entire monster flap is bunk and all the sightings are merely hoaxes. The whole affair, they say, is a plot by local hotel owners and shopkeepers to boost the tourist trade. (Even if the tourist industry of Inverness didn't create the monster, it certainly has taken advantage of its fame. In addition to the scores of postcards, ash trays, dish towels, and commemorative plaques emblazoned with Nessie's picture, you can buy miniature models of the monster to float in your home bathtub. And, if you are hungry, you can stop at the snack bar on the road outside Inverness and have a juicy "monsterburger.")

Sadly enough, in some cases, the claims of fraud are true.

In December, 1933, shortly after the first wave of monster sightings, M. A. Weatherall, a Fellow of the Royal Geographical Society, along with a photographer and a reporter from the London *Daily Mail*, arrived at Loch Ness to conduct their own private investigation.

Within only four days after arrival, the team discovered some strange footprints on the lake shore. Weatherall was so convinced he had found the track of Nessie that he provided this description for the readers of the *Daily Mail*: "It is a four-fingered beast and it has feet or pads eight inches across. I should judge it to be a very soft-footed animal about 20 feet long. The spoor clearly shows the undulations of the pads and the outline of claws and nails. I am convinced it can breathe like a hippopotamus or crocodile with just one nostril out of the water. The spoor I found is only a few hours old, clearly demonstrating that the animal is in the neighborhood where I expected to find it." Unfortunately, Mr. Weatherall failed to notice that both prints seemed to have been made with the same foot.

Plaster casts of the tracks were made and sent to the British Museum of Natural History for positive identification. Two weeks later, the head zoologist of the Museum reported: "We are unable to find any significant difference between these impressions and those made by the foot of a hippopotamus. The closest agreement is with the right hind foot of a mounted specimen, probably not quite full grown."

The zoologist was correct. The prints had been made by two small boys using a stuffed hippopotamus leg that had served as an umbrella stand.

One of the more remarkable photographs of the Loch Ness Monster was taken in 1960 by a 26-year-old fireman named Peter O'Connor. The previous year, O'Connor had attempted to mount a monster-hunting expedition armed with Bren guns, harpoons, underwater spears, and a bomb. Stopped by the local authorities from taking this small arsenal to the loch, he returned alone with only his camera. His photo showed the image of a large, round body some 16 feet long, with an odd appendage sticking out from one end to form a crude neck and head. O'Connor claimed to have shot the photo while standing waist-deep in the loch only 25 yards away from the monster.

Two weeks later, however, a British naturalist visited the spot where O'Connor supposedly had stood. The scientist found the "remains of three large polyurethane bags, a ring of stones each about nine inches in diameter tied together with string, and a long stick." The scientist inflated the plastic bags, weighted them down with stones, wedged the stick in front, and then took a picture that looked identical to O'Connor's monster.

At Foyers, on the southern shore of Loch Ness, the Falls of Foyers drop over the rocky mountainside and cascade through a wooded glen into the loch. Below the falls, there is a stretch of flat shoreline, the site of a small community of lakeside homes, a large aluminum plant, and a few fishing piers. A small trailer with an awning stretched over the doorway stands here too. This is the summer headquarters of Frank Searle, a former British soldier who settled at Loch Ness in 1969 to take up full-time monster hunting.

During his long and lonesome vigil at the lake, Searle has produced a series of pictures of the Loch Ness Monster. These photos are on display outside his trailer and he'll gladly talk to you about them, if you stop. He'll also sell you a set of photos or a copy of his book.

On October 21, 1972, Searle took his best-known pictures. While drifting on the lake in a small dinghy, he heard a great splash and saw the monster appear beside him. He claims to have taken three quick shots of the animal, all showing the creature with its mouth open. The creature then submerged and reappeared 250 yards away and Searle photographed it again, this time as a series of humps. Alas, an examination of the photographs by Loch Ness investigator Nicholas Witchell showed the photos had been retouched. In the one case, an extra hump seems to have been added. Worse yet, under careful study, the "head" appears to have the same shape and contour as a floating oil drum.

Despite these obvious fakes, frauds, and phonies, as well as the unavoidable misconceptions, mistakes, and misinterpretations, a considerable number of both authentic naked-eye observations and photographic records of the Loch Ness Monster do exist.

Professor Roy Mackal estimates there must be at least 10,000 known sightings. And about 3,000 of these observations have been recorded, that is, written down or published in newspapers, books, articles, diaries, and official reports. After examining this written record, Mackal found 251 eyewitness reports that could be considered as positive, significant evidence of some unusual activity in the lake. In other words, over the past 30-40 years, unknown creatures have been seen at least a half dozen times per year at the loch.

Even this relatively low number of annual sightings provides sufficient evidence to suggest some sort of animal, or family of animals, is living in Loch Ness. What is still lacking, however, is sufficient evidence to determine the kind of animal, or animals, it is.

Scientists would like a living specimen to be caught and studied. Even the bones of a deceased monster would be helpful. And if a live specimen or the bodily remains of a dead animal can't be obtained, then researchers at least need a good, clear photograph of the creature.

Unfortunately, for the past 40 years, the monster has remained uncooperative, refusing to be captured either in the flesh or on film. However, it has not been for lack of trying.

A small, but growing band of dedicated researchers, known to the world as "the monster hunters," have patrolled the lake for more than four decades looking for some clue to Nessie's identity. Although the final answer still evades them, there now is hope that a solution may be at hand.

THE SEARCH
BEGINS

An odd crew of men showed up at the labor employment office in Inverness. Craggy-faced Highlanders wearing rough tweed caps and rubber boots came clutching their lunch pails and Kodak cameras. Powerful binoculars hung around their necks. They marched past the desk in single file, stopping briefly to fill out a work form and an insurance card. Each man signed his name; and, under the heading "occupation," they wrote: "Watcher for the Monster."

The first full-scale investigation of the Loch Ness mystery was sponsored in July of 1934 by Sir Edward Mountain, Chairman of the Eagle Star Insurance Company. As a summer resident of the Loch Ness area, he was fascinated by the reports of a large creature in its waters and decided to finance a photographic survey.

Under the direction of Captain James Fraser, 20 unemployed local men were signed up to maintain a daylight surveillance of the lake. Every day for five weeks, the men were taken to positions around the lake where they sat with cameras ready to snap any unusual activity on the surface. Each man would be paid two pounds per week (the equivalent then of about $8), plus a bonus of ten guineas (approximately $40) for anyone who took a successful photograph.

During the five-week expedition, 11 clear visual observations were made, as were several photographs. Perhaps the most interesting sighting was made by P. Grant on August 12, when he saw an object about 20 feet long "appear in the water some 120 yards from shore."

Grant had no glasses or camera with him that day, but "was able to make out clearly the monster's head, which appeared to be like that of a goat. On top of the head were two stumps resembling sheep's horns broken off. The neck was about 40 inches long and where neck and body met appeared considerable swelling which resembled a fowl with a full crop. The color was dark brown on the back and lighter underneath.

The skin appeared smooth with markings like that of a lizard. The animal appeared to have flippers on the fore part of its body. The eyes were mere slits like the eye of a darning needle. [Grant] ... watched the creature for about five minutes and then it submerged, leaving a trail of air bubbles both at the front and rear."

The expedition photos, unfortunately, were not as clear. Four out of the five showed only waves, probably caused by passing boats. One photo, however, showed an elongated dark object partially submerged in the water and apparently throwing up spray as it moved.

After the main crew of monster hunters were laid off, Captain Fraser and an assistant continued their own watch of the loch. On September 15, at 7:15 A.M., as Fraser took up his post near Urquhart Castle, he noticed something three-quarters of a mile away that he described as "an upturned flat-bottomed boat, 15 feet long." Fraser had the presence of mind to turn his motion picture camera on the scene. The resulting 20 feet of film (since lost) was analyzed by zoologists in London, who claimed it was a seal. Fraser was a longtime resident of the loch area and quite familiar with its wildlife. He was convinced he would know a seal when he saw one. And what he had seen was no seal!

Many other smaller private expeditions were launched between 1933 and the end of World War II, but none produced any unusual or significant results. Three of the more interesting sightings came about by chance.

One bright, sunny day in the summer of 1943, a British Navy motor launch was sailing south through the Caledonian Canal en route from Inverness to Fort Augustus, traveling at a top speed of about 25 knots. Suddenly, the crew felt a terrific jolt. Everyone on board was knocked off his feet. Looking forward, the sailors saw a large, dark shape disappearing in a flurry of water. The crew swore that the shape was that of some living thing and not just debris or submerged logs.

On July 14, 1951, Lachlan Stuart, a woodsman living on the south shore of the loch opposite Urquhart Castle, arose early to milk his cow.

Looking out the window, he saw what appeared to be a boat speeding down the middle of the lake. But this boat had a strange hump! He grabbed his small box camera and rushed outdoors and down the hill to the bank. As he focused his camera, he saw three humps in the viewfinder, and he snapped his shot. The three humps remained visible as the beast continued swimming on. At one point, a long, thin neck and head about the size of a sheep's appeared in front of the humps, but he did not capture this on film.

Stuart's film remains one of the clearest ever taken of the monster, showing the distinctive shape of the humps. However, close examination reveals that the humps are really three separate objects, apparently unconnected. This suggests to many investigators that Stuart actually had photographed a group of animals rather than only one.

One of the most productive modern investigation techniques at Loch Ness owes its introduction to a fishing boat. On the morning of December 2, 1954, the drifter *Rival III* was sailing down the loch headed for the West Coast fishing grounds. As the boat approached Urquhart Castle, the first mate glanced at the ship's sonar screen and couldn't believe his eyes. (Sonar is an electronic device often used by fishermen to locate schools of fish or dangerous shoals and reefs by listening to the echoes of radio beams bounced off these underwater objects.) The printer arm on his recording machine had gone wild. The graph showed the shape of some large, fast-moving object below the ship. Once back in port, the chart was analyzed and studied. It showed an object some 50 feet long traveling in the same direction as the boat at a depth of about 480 feet. The signal indicated it was a single, large object and not a school of fish moving together. Although this experience should have proved the potential of sonar as a tool for searching the lake, no other serious attempts at sonar investigations would be made for 14 years.

In the meantime, many determined and dedicated amateurs continued their vigil at Loch Ness. For some of these amateurs, like Tim Dinsdale, the search would become an obsession. In April, 1960, Dinsdale was driving leisurely along the southern shore of the lake when he spotted a long oval shape, dark brown except for some black blotches on the hind parts, lying motionless in the water. For some reason, as he later wrote in his own book on the Loch Ness Monster, the shape reminded him of an African buffalo. Then, abruptly, the shape began to move. "I saw ripples break away from the further end," wrote Dinsdale, "and I knew I was looking at the extraordinary humped back of some huge living creature!"

Dinsdale grabbed the 16 mm Bolex movie camera sitting on the car seat beside him and began filming the object as it moved in a zig-zag path across the loch. Dinsdale filmed for about four minutes; then, gambling that the creature might come closer to shore, he drove madly down the road to a point where the highway came close to the bank. By the time he arrived, the creature had gone. Fortunately, Dinsdale already had 50 feet of clear, well-focused film. The film remains one of the best documentary records of unusual activity in Loch Ness.

For Dinsdale, this film was also the start of a new career. He quit his job as an aeronautical engineer in Britain and moved to Scotland, where he has remained ever since, attempting to photograph the elusive lake creature again. Take warning from his example: Monster hunting can be habit-forming!

DRAWING IN
THE NET

Night at Loch Ness. Darkness beyond belief. Black as the inside of a felt glove. Low-hanging clouds shroud the surrounding hills. No stars penetrate the gloom. On the far shore, a few orange and yellow pinpoints twinkle faintly — the lights of scattered houses, or perhaps the lanterns of poachers prowling the wooded banks.

Suddenly, a blinding flash! A bright beam of white light sweeps across the inky waters. Back and forth the powerful beam swings, skimming the loch's surface. For an hour or more the light slowly traces a pattern up and down the center of the lake.

What's that? The beam halts. Retreats slightly. A thin "fingerlike object" pokes six or eight feet out of the water many yards from the shore. For a moment, both beam and object are motionless, the strange "finger" shining brighter than the surrounding waves. Then, the object — whatever it was! — disappears beneath the surface.

For two weeks in 1962, with the help of Britain's Associated Television network, the Loch Ness Investigation Bureau used war surplus searchlights to scan the loch for any signs of Nessie's nighttime activity.

On the night of October 19, they made that intriguing observation of a "finger" poking out of the loch. By coincidence, early that same day, seven expedition members also saw and filmed "a long, dark shape" moving some 200 yards offshore from Urquhart Bay. The presence of the shape in the water also visibly disturbed fish in the loch.

A month later, an independent committee studied the findings of the Bureau and concluded that: "There is some unidentified animate object in Loch Ness which, if it be a mammal, amphibian, reptile, fish, or mollusk of any known order, is of such a size as to be worthy of careful scientific examination and identification."

The Loch Ness Investigation Bureau was founded in 1962 by two naturalists: Sir Peter Scott, son of the famous Antarctic explorer and himself the founder of the International Wildfowl Trust; and Richard Fitter, a member of the Fauna Preservation Society. They, in turn, won the support of David James, an explorer, World War II hero, and a member of British Parliament from the Highland area.

With this distinguished backing, but little money, the Bureau established summer headquarters along the loch. For the next decade, the Bureau mustered large teams of observers who produced scores of visual sightings. During the rest of the year, the Bureau served as a clearinghouse for other information and observations made by all sources — both amateur and professional. Eventually, the Bureau built up a valuable and impressive file of eyewitness reports.

Perhaps encouraged by the credentials of the Bureau founders, other British and American researchers began taking a more serious look at the Loch Ness phenomenon in the late 1960's.

In the summer of 1968, the use of sonar became a regular part of the investigations. Sonar is a form of underwater radar first developed during World War II as a device for locating submarines. A radio transmitter sends out a very high frequency sound wave which bounces off distant objects and returns to the sender. The time it takes for the sound wave to travel out and return gives an accurate indication of the distance or depth of the object. With modifications, sonar systems can also be used to show the shape and size of an underwater object and to determine its rate of travel. Usually, the receiver listening to the radio echoes is linked to a pen on a graph paper, so variations in the ink tracings will describe the rough dimensions of an object and its direction of motion.

Professor D. G. Tucker, Head of the Department of Electronic and Electrical Engineering at the University of Birmingham, England, felt the loch was a perfect testing ground for some new sonar equipment he had developed.

The sonar device was installed at Temple Pier near Drumnadrochit on Loch Ness's north shore. The narrow beams were trained straight out into the loch to a range of about 700 yards. Thus, they established a "sonar gate" through which any moving object — or creature — would have to pass to reach suspected feeding grounds.

If any object passed through this "sonar gate," the movement would be detected and the "blips" or tracings on the sonar screen could be photographed.

On the afternoon of August 28, the sonar picked up the echo of a "large object," perhaps 150 feet long, less than half a mile from shore. For nearly ten minutes, the object crossed and recrossed the beam, rising and diving at speeds up to 120 feet per minute.

Then, the first object was joined by two others. An analysis of the sonar record suggested one of these objects could be a school of fish. But the third object behaved in an extremely unusual fashion, unlike any known fish. This object reached speeds of 15 knots and dove with a velocity of 450 feet per minute.

Could the two large diving objects have been unknown creatures in pursuit of the school of fish?

The sonar system merely gives rough size and speed; it cannot describe details of form or shape. Although Dr. Tucker made no claims to have discovered a monster, longtime observers at Loch Ness felt he had found the first good evidence of large creatures in the deep. At the same time, many members of the scientific community ridiculed his findings. However, enough people took the sonar sightings seriously to justify further experiments.

The following summer, with support from the publishers of *World Book Encyclopedia*, the Loch Ness Investigation Bureau launched an expedition that had long been dreamed of by everyone associated with the mystery: exploration by a manned submarine.

Loch Ness had never seen anything like it! The tiny, one-man, bright yellow submarine looked almost too small to venture out in the depths of the lake. Designed, built, and piloted by Dan Taylor of Atlanta, Georgia, the *Viperfish* would patrol the loch underwater and then zoom in and track any strange objects picked up by a sonar system operated from a boat on the surface. Alas, despite the high hopes of its sponsors, *Viperfish* was not equal to the task of exploring the great depths and distances of Loch Ness. After experiencing numerous technical difficulties — on one occasion the submarine was gripped and spun about by a mysterious force on the loch bottom — the expedition was abandoned.

By coincidence, a second submarine was at Loch Ness that summer. The *Pisces* had arrived there with a movie company to assist in the filming of the movie *The Private. Lives of Sherlock Holmes*. The submarine would tow one of the movie props — a five-ton, dummy "monster" — out into the lake so that the model would appear to be swimming under its own power. But bad luck plagued everyone that summer. As the model was being towed out for its first scene, the tow line snapped and the mock monster sank immediately to the bottom. (Some skeptics of the Loch Ness investigation effort say *we now can be sure of at least one monster in the lake!*)

Free from its movie-making duties, the *Pisces* made a number of practice dives, including one to 820 feet, or some 70 feet deeper than had previously been measured at Loch Ness. Below 750 feet, the crew reported seeing strange colored eels and experiencing powerful currents.

One day, while hovering only 50 feet above the bottom in the loch's main channel, 300 yards north of Urquhart Castle, the crew spotted a large object on their own sonar. The submarine began to move toward the object. But, as the *Pisces* drew within 400 feet, the object suddenly disappeared from the screen. What was it? No one knows.

Despite the disappointments and near misses, the Loch Ness researchers were not discouraged. In fact, they were highly encouraged. The underwater sonar observations of 1968 and 1969 had provided solid confirmation that something could exist beneath the surface. And these sightings could not be dismissed as hoaxes or optical illusions. The investigators would return to Loch Ness again.

THE FIRST
BREAKTHROUGHS

The man in the front of the small boat sat hunched over a radio receiver twiddling with the dials. A long insulated line ran from the receiver over the gunwales of the boat into water. A set of earphones were clamped tightly on his head. His partner sat on the rear, tending the slow-idling outboard motor.

A puzzled look crossed the face of the man at the radio. He had picked up some strange clicking sounds much like the chirping of birds. The sounds came from all directions, perhaps from several sources. They rose and fell in intensity, sometimes becoming loud enough to drown out all other sounds from the lake.

"Suddenly," Roy Mackal wrote later, "we realized that these were not mechanical sounds, but calls produced by living creatures in the water below. Alone in the small boat with darkness falling, it was an awesome feeling. Somewhere nearby were unseen animals calling to each other."

In the summer of 1970, Roy Mackal and the Loch Ness Investigation Bureau, again with support from *World Book Encyclopedia*, mounted one of the most intense expeditions ever conducted at Loch Ness. In addition to the continued use of sonar surveys, elaborate underwater camera systems were installed to photograph anything swimming in the waters, and, most interesting, a series of hydrophones were installed at various locations around the lake. Microphones and recording equipment were suspended inside huge, watertight oil drums.

During that summer, four unusual recordings were made, including a series of "clicks and knocks" coming in regular patterns and apparently stopping whenever a boat approached the spot where they originated. Mackal and others interpreted these sounds as communication between creatures in the deep waters.

That summer of 1970 also marked the arrival of a new investigation team that would eventually set the scientific world on its ear by producing the most convincing evidence for the existence of large living creatures in the loch.

Robert H. Rines is a Boston patent lawyer. He is also the head of the Academy of Applied Science, a private research organization founded in 1963 to explore those areas of science ignored or shunned by conventional researchers. In 1969, after hearing Roy Mackal describe his monster searches, Rines decided to lend the support of his organization to the hunt.

The Rines team included Martin Klein, developer of side-scan sonar, a modification of the depth-finding device that allows radio beams to be sent horizontally across a body of water rather than only straight downward into its depths.

Rines and Klein planned two approaches to their search. First, they would use the side-scan sonar to monitor sections of the loch where the creatures might feed. Second, with the help of biologists at American universities, and government agencies, they developed "artificial attractants" that might appeal to the senses of the creature. These attractants, or "bait," would be trailed behind a slow-moving boat together with an underwater camera. If Nessie swam up to nibble on the bait, it would have its picture snapped.

Although the world's press made a great

fuss over the use of "attractants," calling them "sex lures" and "monster perfumes," this aspect of the expedition met with little success. However, the sonar system did produce some interesting results. On September 21, the sonar installed at the end of Temple Pier detected two large objects swimming through the beam. Seconds later, one of the objects returned through the beam. Tantalizing evidence of a large and fast-moving object beneath the water again had been found.

Encouraged by this initial success, the Academy of Applied Science team returned to the loch yearly. Robert Rines even bought a small cottage on the shore as a permanent base for his summer operations. And he added a new tool to his arsenal of monster-seeking devices: underwater electronic strobescopic cameras.

A strobescopic camera is one equipped with a super-bright flashgun. The flashes are timed so precisely that extremely fast photographs can be made to "stop motion."

The underwater version of the strobe camera was developed by Professor Harold Edgerton of MIT for use by marine explorer Jacques Cousteau in undersea adventures. Edgerton is sometimes called "Papa Flash" because of his camera invention. His strobe cameras have been used to photograph everything from atomic bomb blasts to stop-motion records of falling water drops.

At Loch Ness, the flash camera system was mounted beneath the loch's surface in watertight cylinders. Since the lights flashed simultaneously with each advance of the film, each frame was brilliantly illuminated. The photographic equipment was operated along with the sonar, so images on one system could be confirmed by records on the other.

On the night of August 7, 1972, the crew on the boat tending the two systems noticed some pinpoints on the sonar screen. This was interpreted as salmon on their annual migration through the lake. Then, about 1:45 A.M., the dots became streaks. The fish, apparently frightened, were speeding away from something in the area. A big, dark trace appeared on the screen. It grew and grew in size until it became many times that of the fish. No one could imagine what was down below. But, if it had been seen on sonar, then it must have been captured on film as well.

The color films and sonar tracing were flown within a few days to the United States. The film was developed under bond at the main offices of Eastman Kodak, so there could be no suspicion of tampering.

At first, the films seemed disappointing. Although four frames showed hazy outlines of some large and solid objects, the peat-stained waters of the loch badly blurred the outlines. The photos were then sent to NASA's photo-enhancement experts, the same team that has used computer techniques to improve the images of the Viking pictures sent from Mars. This technique does not change a photo in any way, it merely improves the clarity by sharpening shades and tones of color and providing an interpretation of any missing sections.

One enhanced picture showed something remarkable: a portion of a rough-textured body with a large flipper or fin attached to its midsection. The photographic experts who examined the film estimated the flipper as six to eight feet long and two to four feet wide. In another picture taken 15 seconds later, a long tail-like structure at least 80 feet long was seen. Most significant, the photographic evidence could be matched with the sonar sighting.

Dr. George Zug of the Smithsonian Institution examined the photos and agreed they showed "a flipperlike structure . . . attached to a robust body." Zug also felt it had the same shape as the tail of the palmate newt.

Officials of the New England Aquarium who viewed the pictures stated: "It does not appear mammalian. The general shape and form of the flipper does not fit anything known today."

Had Nessie been found? Many scientific experts were still skeptical. They felt more proof was needed. More photographs or, better yet, a live specimen. "Show us the monster, then we'll believe it."

Robert Rines and his team returned to Loch Ness to find the additional evidence the scientists demanded.

NESSIE
REVEALED

The distinguished members of Parliament sat in stunned silence. The pictures they had just seen were mind-boggling. One photo showed a thick-bodied, long-necked creature with a small reptilelike head emerging from a murky blue background. The other, even more remarkable, showed a huge grotesque head with a gaping mouth, and strange hornlike appendages sprouting above a single, dark, evil eye.

The British House of Commons had met in special session on December 10, 1975, to witness the unveiling of a monster . . . the Loch Ness Monster!

After the success of the combined sonar-camera observations, Robert Rines and his

American Academy of Applied Science crew returned to Loch Ness for two more summers in hopes of filming the creature again. On June 20, 1975, they got their photos!

Two camera systems were being used that summer. In addition to the original system of strobe lights mated with a 16 mm motion picture camera, Doc Edgerton had devised a new system that used sonar to trigger the filming. In other words, when something passed through the sonar beam, the cameras started rolling. But something went wrong with that new system. And, it was the old faithful camera that captured the most intriguing images.

The film from June 20 has many normal frames; that is, lots of murky water devoid of any life except for a few fish. But sometime in the early morning, the camera also snapped a very special photo. The film shows a large, gray body, its shape outlined roughly by the strobe light against an inky background of dark lake water. Two triangular flippers, or fins, hang down the middle of this body. A long, arched neck stretches upward. A small head appears connected to this neck, even though a gap of water separates the two features.

A second frame on this film record is equally striking. The distinct shape of a boat is silhouetted against a bright background. Obviously, the camera somehow had been knocked about and twisted around so it pointed straight up to photograph the bottom of the research boat. Could something — the creature, perhaps — have bumped into the camera?

Then, two frames later, came the most spectacular picture of all!

"It looks like a cabbage," said one researcher getting his first glimpse. To a casual observer, the photo can be puzzling. But, on closer examination, the object can be seen to have perfect symmetry, that is, its two sides have identical and matching features, a quality found only in living things. With a little more imagination, you can also see an eye, an open mouth, nostrils, and hornlike protuberances. No mistaking it, this was the head of a real creature!

What happened that day? How was Nessie's picture snapped? Apparently, the creature swam past the camera early in the day; later, it returned, bumping into the camera device and sending it flying upward. Then, perhaps angered, hurt, even frightened, Nessie dove at the camera with teeth bared, ready to attack!

These photos, like the others taken earlier by Rines's group, were sent to the NASA film experts for enhancement and analysis.

After an extensive computer study, Alan Gillespie of the Jet Propulsion Lab reported: "One picture shows a body with a long neck and two sturdy appendages . . . the second frame appears to show a neck and head, with the head closer to the camera than the body. The neck is reticulated [covered with a fishnet pattern of lines]. The head supports projections.

"I see no evidence they are pictures of a model, toy, or whatever," Gillespie emphasized. "I detect no evidence of fraud. These objects are not patterns of algae, sediment, or gas bubbles."

Such photos were sure to cause a sensation in the scientific community and an uproar in the popular press. They most certainly did!

Rines and his colleagues had planned to announce their results at a serious scientific conference in Edinburgh, Scotland, in early December. Premature publication of news about the photos caused such an uproar that the investigators canceled their planned program.

Instead, they published their photos in the prestigious British scientific journal *Nature*. At the same time, they gave a special presentation for the House of Commons. The researchers asked the British lawmakers to protect and preserve the creature of Loch Ness — whatever it might be — under the National Conservation of Wildlife Act. To meet the requirements of this law, Rines and Peter Scott (sponsor of past expeditions and now chairman of the World Wildlife Fund) gave the creature the scientific name: *Nessiteras rhombopteryx*, which means "the Ness marvel with the diamond-shaped fin."

Suddenly, scientists around the world started taking the Loch Ness Monster more seriously.

Dr. Christopher McGowan of the Royal Ontario Museum wrote: "I am satisfied there is sufficient evidence to support the theory that there is an unexplained phenomenon of considerable interest in Loch Ness. The evidence suggests the presence of large aquatic animals."

A. W. Crompton, a Harvard biologist, commented: "I personally find the photographs extremely intriguing and sufficiently suggestive of a large aquatic animal to both urge and recommend that more intensive investigations be undertaken."

Perhaps the most positive support came from Dr. George Zug of the Smithsonian, who was convinced that "the data indicate the presence of large animals in Loch Ness."

Zug wouldn't attempt a positive identification on the basis of the photos alone, but he would speculate on the size and nature of the creature and on the possible numbers that might live in the lake.

For an animal the size suggested by the photos (about 20 feet long), Zug claimed it would have a growth period of nearly 20 years. Because creatures of various size had been seen for 40 years — indeed, 1,400 years! — he felt there probably was, and always had been, more than just *one* "Loch Ness Monster." (Of course, if only a single creature had produced all those sightings since St. Columba's day, the poor animal would be rather old and decrepit by now!)

The actual number of creatures in the lake would depend on the amount of food available for them. Considerable disagreement exists about how many fish are in the lake, with estimates ranging from a few hundred thousand tons to several million tons of salmon, Arctic char, and eels. (Some monster-hunters have been severely criticized for overestimating the fish population of Loch Ness. According to one naturalist, if there were as many fish as Professor Mackal has suggested, then one could walk across the lake on the backs of the salmon stuffed in the water.)

Even based on the most conservative estimates, Zug still feels there are probably enough fish to support a colony of ten to 20 monsters, each weighing 3,000 pounds. On the other hand, if the creatures weighed only 300 pounds each, there could be as many as 150 of them in Loch Ness.

But what is this creature? The pictures certainly show something that has roughly the same shape and size as the plesiosaur. Is it really a prehistoric beast that has managed to survive in Loch Ness?

Not everyone is convinced the cameras have found a living fossil. Some skeptics claim the photos are merely cases of mistaken identity. The "body" of Nessie is really an old Viking ship, they say, and the fins hanging down its sides are oars. The "head" is the carving of a dragon on its bowsprit.

Other critics claim the "head" is the rotting carcass of a Highland stag or old cow that fell in the lake, or merely a clump of peat moss or gas bubbles. Someone even suggested that the Rines research team photographed the missing movie monster that sank in Loch Ness six years earlier.

Rines and the Academy of Applied Science vowed to eliminate any lingering doubts. They would return to Loch Ness and bring back even better photographs. In the summer of 1976, they did return — and so did half the world!

DISAPPOINTMENT
IN 1976

"Loch Ness never gives up its secrets," the old Scottish farmer solemnly told me. We stood in the shadow of the ruined Urquhart Castle, gazing out over the wind-tossed water. "The bodies of people who drown in the loch are never found," he added, and I shivered slightly, perhaps from the cool mist that fell on us. Or perhaps it was the mixed sense of dread and wonder I felt here beside this dark lake and its shattered reminder of ancient clan warfare.

One of the questions asked most often about the Loch Ness Monster is: Why have no remains of the creature ever been found? Surely, if large creatures live in the loch, they must die there too. Why do we find no bones or bodies washed up on the shore?

The answer to this riddle lies in the lake's cool and constant temperature. About 150 feet below the surface, the temperature is always around 42 degrees Fahrenheit, winter and summer. At this temperature, bodies decompose slowly. The gases that usually form rapidly in decaying carcasses are produced at a much lower rate. Instead of bloating up and popping to the surface, bodies sink to the bottom of the lake. The soft parts of the flesh are eaten by eels and other fish and the heavier bones simply settle on the lake bed. Here they lay undisturbed, gently covered by thin layers of sifting silt, peat particles, and sand.

A search of the lake bottom thus should reveal the bones of dead Loch Ness creatures. Such a search would be a major goal of the Academy of Applied Science's 1976 expedition. Special side-scan sonar devices developed by Klein Associates would be towed behind boats patrolling slowly over the lake's surface. The yellow, torpedo-shaped, sonar "fish" would send out rapid, high-frequency sound pulses that would bounce off the lake bottom and back to receivers on the boat. On the chart recorders, any large structures or objects on the lake bottom would appear as dark traces, with their shape and size clearly outlined.

Before leaving the United States, the

team tested the device by scattering some mastodon bones on the floor of a pond in New Hampshire. The sonar device located and clearly defined these "test bones."

In addition, another sonar system would be set up at the Academy's summer site on Temple Pier, scanning the entrance to Urquhart Bay, a suspected feeding ground for the creatures and the same spot where the spectacular 1975 photos had been taken. And, again, the sonar would be linked to underwater camera systems. This summer, too, the team would use three flash-camera systems, plus an underwater television camera that could be monitored continuously. If anything appeared on the screen, the operator would simply push a button and Polaroid cameras would snap the television screen images and two of the underwater cameras would be activated to take simultaneous stereographic photos of the creature. Because the investigators suspected the flashing light on the camera the year before had attracted the creature, the older camera would be used as "bait" and its flash photography would be increased from once every 1.4 minutes to once every 15 seconds.

In charge of the filming operation was Charles Wyckoff, a photographic expert who had developed special films for other impossible tasks, such as photographing nuclear blasts and solar eclipses. Wyckoff also made the first analysis of the now-famous 1975 films. In addition to Robert Rines and Doc Edgerton, the talent-packed team included sonar experts Marty Klein and Charles Finkelstein, Canadian biologist Chris McGowan, television specialist Ike Blondar, plus a host of student volunteers, research assistants, and visiting consultants in electronics, biology, and marine survey. Obviously, it would be the most sophisticated expedition ever mounted at Loch Ness. The operation was funded in part by *The New York Times*, which claimed exclusive publication rights to any major discoveries.

The *Times* reporters had a hard time defending their exclusive coverage, however. A horde of reporters from other newspapers and television stations around the world — all attracted by the 1975 photos and the promise of a final solution to the monster mystery — also arrived at Loch Ness in June. NBC came with a film crew. So did the British Broadcasting Corporation. The *National Geographic* sent its top underwater photography team. Bob Cooke, the *Boston Globe*'s crack science writer, attempting to scoop the *Times*, also came. Even cartoonist Garry Trudeau, creator of the "Doonesbury" comic strip, arrived to record the more lighthearted aspects of the research.

The whole world waited for news from Loch Ness. But something funny happened on the way to the lake. Nessie didn't show up for the interview!

When I arrived at Loch Ness in mid-July, many of the news people had already packed up for home, bored by the lack of action on the lake. A few writers and photographers were still staying at the Drumnadrochit Hotel, but I could sense their disappointment.

The next day, I drove down to Temple Pier, about a mile away. Charlie Wyckoff met me at the door of the lakeside house that he and his wife and another expedition couple had rented for the summer.

"Come on in and have some toast," he said. It was ten-thirty and Charlie had just gotten up. "We were out on the lake until four this morning," he explained. "We haven't had any daytime successes, so we are now trying night operations."

So far, the nighttime trolling hadn't been any more successful. As we sat looking out over the lake, the sun was shining brightly and houses could be seen clearly on the distant shore. Scores of pleasure boats cruised gaily up and down the calm surface of the lake.

"We've had a lot of problems, and those are some of them," he said, pointing toward the boats. "There is more boat traffic, mainly tourists, on the lake this summer than ever before. Perhaps it's keeping the animals down deep in the water. We don't know."

Another more serious problem seemed to be the lack of fish in the loch. An epidemic disease among Atlantic salmon the previous summer had severely reduced the salmon population throughout the British Isles. Now the unusually dry summer (which also caused serious drought problems in all of Northern Europe) had delayed the normal migration period of the salmon. The fish population in the lake was far below normal. Without fish to feed on, the mysterious animals, too, had become scarce. No surface sightings had been made. If the lake monsters were still in Loch Ness, they were avoiding the shallow waters near shore and remaining at great depths in the center of the lake.

In an attempt to improve their photographic chances, the Academy team had moved the camera systems to a point about 700 yards off Temple Pier, where the water was deeper. A variety of mechanical problems also plagued the operation: unavailability of spare parts, water seepage into the underwater canisters, lack of suitable film processing facilities. Still, even when these problems were solved, no animals showed up to be photographed.

The sonar system had proved its worth, however. Wyckoff took me down to a small trailer parked by the pier. Crammed with electronic gear, wires, tubes, and canisters of film, the trailer served as a mobile laboratory and nerve center for the expedition. Wyckoff showed me some sonar echoes made on the night of June 30.

On that night, a large object had swum in front of the pier. The exact shape cannot be discerned from the sonar chart, for it appears only as a large, dark blob among many other smaller blobs that seem to be fish. However, the larger blob had moved quite rapidly and almost deliberately toward the equipment suspended under the water. Then, suddenly, it veered away and sped off out of range, again, at a relatively fast rate.

"It had to be a living creature," said Wyckoff. "No drifting object, like a log or clump of peat moss, could make that pattern. Unfortunately, we had camera problems, so we didn't get any pictures. But we watched the surface of the lake at the same time and there were no boats passing when this object appeared on the chart. It had to be something big — and alive — under the water."

The other sonar system searching for the bones of Nessie had little success. Perhaps the depths of Loch Ness are just too great. However, the sonar team stumbled on another unexpected discovery that may be equally important to science.

While gliding over a shallow bay near the village of Lochend, the sonar detected a complex of large, prehistoric, man-made stoneworks on the floor of the lake. The stone complex included a long wall and several large cairns, or burial mounds. Such ruins have been found throughout Great Britain; in fact, the hills around Loch Ness are dotted with these stone piles. But most were plundered of any valuable relics centuries ago. By contrast, the ancient structures found on the lake floor may never have been touched by grave robbers. If this settlement was suddenly covered by rising lake water 2,000 to 3,000 years ago, the contents of the cairns may be undisturbed. Thus the search for the monster may have an unusual fringe benefit for archeologists: a perfectly sealed and preserved sample of ancient culture.

The sonar team also found the remains of a training plane that crashed in the lake during World War II. But no sign of Nessie or her cousins.

By the end of the summer of 1976, as the days grew shorter and colder and the first signs of color appeared in the forests around Loch Ness, the scientific team dismantled its gear and headed for home. The newspaper and television reporters had long since left for other assignments. And the final tour buses made their slow circuits of the lake, stopping briefly above Urquhart Bay to point out the spot where Nessie had been seen and photographed.

Had those 1975 pictures, which seemed so promising as the final clues to Nessie's identity, been only flukes? Could any large creature — or family of creatures — really remain undetected for so long from so many determined hunters? Are the skeptics right? Is the search only a wild goose chase? Or, are the Loch Ness animals really throwbacks to the prehistoric period, great intelligent beasts that deliberately avoid detection? Will Loch Ness ever give up its secrets? Your guess is as good as anyone's!

MORE ABOUT
THE MONSTER

Baumann, E.D. *The Loch Ness Monster*; Franklin Watts, New York, 1973.

Costello, Peter. *In Search of Lake Monsters*; Berkeley, New York, 1976.

Dinsdale, Tim. *Monster Hunt*; Acropolis Books, Washington, 1972.

Heuvelmans, Bernard. *In the Wake of the Sea Serpents*; Hill and Wang, New York, 1968.

Holiday, F.W. *The Dragon and the Disc*; W. W. Norton, New York, 1976.

Mackal, Roy P. *The Monsters of Loch Ness;* Swallow Press, Chicago, 1976.

Witchell, Nicholas. *The Loch Ness Story*; Penguin, London, 1976.